The Ultimate Guide

To Saving Money on

Electricity

By

Jack Daytona

Table of Contents

Foreword

It comes every month...

You pull into the driveway after another hellish day at your thankless job. All you want to do is go inside, grab a beverage, plant your ass on the couch, tune out and watch the game or binge watch that series all your co-workers keep bullying you for not watching.

You crack open the door of your geriatric car and try to keep your eyes focused on the front door of your home. You engage your 'out-of-fucks to give' tunnel vision, deliberately avoiding eye contact with the weeds and the overgrown grass that's beginning to swallow the kid's toys.

It been a long day and those twenty feet between the driveway and the house are all that separate you from another blissful evening of eyestrain and brain-rot. You take the first step, but something stops you. A feeling of malice builds up in your core, and you have the distinct feeling of being watched. "Where is that feeling coming from?"

You glance down at the garden gnome who is giving you the finger and a fatherly look of disapproval for letting his home turn into an urban apocalypse. A faint voice of responsibility begins whispering your name. You scan the scene around you and spot the culprit immediately. The mailbox!

The end of the month has come again. You've successfully avoided the inevitable evil that now lurks in your mailbox waiting you strike fear into your wallet. But you can't avoid it any longer. It's time for you to put on your big boy pants and face the music.

Taking one slow, dogged step after another, you make your way across the yard, dodging the land mines from the neighbor's dog—*that fucking cocker spaniel.* Reaching the edge of this suburban wilderness, you stand, face-to-face with the heart-of-darkness.

You quickly pull back the lid, and your heart sinks; it's stuffed to the brim. Paper of every color assaults your eyes. You can't even slide your cowardly fingers between the contents and its metal hull to dislodge the evil envelope of terror from its dark lair. You manage to remove the five pounds of fliers, credit-card offers, and bullshit magazines you stopped reading years ago but never canceled. You don't see it at first. Your heart lifts a millimeter in your stomach. "Maybe it isn't there," you hope against hope.

Maybe the electric company decided to have mercy on you after the financial enema they gave you last month. Maybe there was a mistake in the billing department, and they added your bill to your dipshit neighbor's. *Serves him right for not picking up after his Cocker Spaniel*, you think to yourself as you step just a little more briskly on your way back across the yard, toward your front-door.

You enter the house, grab and uncap a frosty beverage, and plant yourself smugly down into the hollow you've so carefully crafted in your recliner. You begin thumbing through the stack of mail-trash, tossing the articles into various piles according to their specific uselessness—and then you see it. There, at the bottom of the heap—right next to where your heart has now sunk—is the electric bill.

"Fuck!" you yell.

After a few minutes of convulsion, you slowly recover yourself. Maybe there is a silver lining. Maybe it isn't so bad. This bill *is* for October, after all. You should be through the worst months, right? This new-found hope in hand, you tear the envelope open and extract the one page from the fifty-page bundle that actually means anything—the account summary.

But no silver-lining awaits you. A pain seems to issue out from the page itself and travels up your arm before lodging itself into your brain. It's higher... The bill is higher... "How in the fucking, fuckity, fuck, fuck is the bill higher than last month?"

How indeed, my friend. How indeed.

Does this scenario sound familiar to you? Are you one of the millions of Americans that feel like they have no control over that tyrannical overlord that is the electric company? Do you find yourself wondering, month after month, how something invisible can cost so much, and how you might be able to change that fate?

If you answered "Yes!" to any or all of these questions, know that you are not alone. We stand with you in solidarity against the evils of the electric company. Keep reading, friend. Within these pages, we have gathered for you the keys to fixing your broken relationship with your mailbox; to softening that monthly jolt to your bank account and sanity. In this book, are the secrets to lowering your electric bill.

How to Read This

...with the lights on (ironically) and a sense of humor squarely intact. Seriously, this is intended to be informative. And by the end, you will be able to use the information you've learned to save a shocking amount on your monthly electric bill.

That said, we're also trying to have a little fun here. Unless you're a direct descendant of Thomas Edison, you probably don't get too amped up about electricity. So, we hope we've written this with enough wit, sarcasm and puns to keep you fully charged up about the subject.

Is that cool? Cool! Now, sit back, relax and prepare for a crash course in saving money. Let's get zapping!

Chapter 1: Admitting You Have a Problem

Sex with lights out make electricity last long time.
—Zen (ish) proverb

Before we dive in too deep, I guess it makes sense to set some ground rules. We really aren't dealing with too complicated of a topic, here, right? I mean if you want to save money on electricity, there are really only two headings that the various strategies can fall under: use less of it; or pay less for it. That's it.

Now, we're going to talk about all kinds of clever methods. We'll be in the house, out of the house. Big stuff, small stuff. Complex, simple. Expensive, free. And every bit of it is going to boil down to those two overall goals.

Use less or pay less.

Getting excited? Great! But, before you go running around the property on an unplugging rampage, let's have a quick education on where most of your electricity is going.

Biggest Offenders

Heating and Cooling

In 1902, the first modern electrical air-conditioning unit was invented by Willis Carrier of Buffalo, New York. Thanks to Mr. Carrier, people have been able to comfortably move to and live in places throughout the world, that their "western" sensibilities had there-to-fore only scoffed at.

Also, thanks to this bringer of comfort, our electric bills have been soaring ever since. Worth it? Probably, but we're going to give you some strategies on how to beat the heat (and the cold) without beating your bank account so much in the process.

The Water Heater

Another modern convenience, the water heater allows us to bathe in comfort, wash our clothes effectively, and bring our tea to boil more quickly. But at what cost? I'll tell you what cost—a huge one! All this convenience, has our budgets in hot water... I'm sorry, I really couldn't resist. But, fear not. These hidden boilers don't have to be hidden money spenders.

Washer and Dryer

Churning, spinning, beeping, rocking, heating... What do these have in common? All of it takes energy. And what does energy take? That's right, dollars! Follow are advice and pull your laundry room back from its money laundering ways. We'll also help you take some of your time back in the process.

The Lights

We know you like to see when it's dark out. Who doesn't? Heck, I'm sitting in we well-lit room as I type. But that doesn't mean there isn't a bunch of ways to reduce the amount of electricity you're using on those lights. Stick around and we'll show you how you might even be able to tap into better lighting while reducing your spend.

The Fridge and the Oven

Keeping food cool and making it hot— both of these things are hugely important to your health and happiness. You'd have to travel far and look pretty hard to find any modern kitchen without both a refrigerator and a stove. But both of these helpers are also costing you dearly—and they really don't have to be. Chances are you are using them wrong and maintaining them poorly. I'm sorry to be so hard on you, but them's the facts, sir. Now if your pride is still intact, I'll show you how to reverse the trend.

Not unplugging things when they're not in use

Uh, DUH! Right? But seriously, how many times have you left that bathroom light on, or left the space heater plugged in, or woken up in the middle of the night to find your kid passed out on the couch with seventeen gaming devices surrounding his fast-asleep ass? It may seem like these would only waste trivial amounts of energy, and you'd be right. But all these little things add up. And isn't it about doing the right thing in the first place? No? It's just about the money? Fine, at least you'll have a good reason to yell at your son for rotting his brain on those video games, right?

Track Your Electric Usage

Another little tidbit you should consider before we get too far, is that you don't have to wait for your electric bill to see how much power you've used. There are tons of ways to do this, from whole-house monitoring systems that you can keep up with right from your phone, to simple power strips that help you stay aware of how much sizzle-juice you're using on specific devices and appliances.

Being aware of how much electricity you use is a great first step to saving money. Once you're aware, you'll be more sensitive to saving, and therefor naturally take all of the steps we cover in this book to reduce your energy consumption, right? Awesome. So, get an app, use a spreadsheet, write it down on a legal pad, buy a whole-house system. I don't care how you track it, just fucking start, okay? Awesome! Now let's take a look at that electric bill, and what in the holy fuck it means in the first place.

Chapter 2: My Favorite Childhood Memory is Not Paying Bills

When you were young, you were afraid of the dark. Now, when you get your electric bill, you're afraid of the light.
—adult word porn

Electricity bills can be a veritable brain-punch of confusion, and most people don't risk the headache of straying past that one number next to "Amount Due." But understanding the rest of the mystery can actually give you some clues to reducing your monthly electrical usage, and therefore, saving you money.

Now that you've survived the initial jolt upon opening the dreaded envelope-of-hate—and seeing that ridiculous number at the top—let's help you understand exactly what all those other numbers are.

Usage

This one is pretty straight-forward. How much electricity did your entertainment and comfort-hungry family use over the last billing period?

It's measured in (kWh), which stands for kilowatt hours. A kilowatt is one thousand watts, and an hour is ... well, an hour of time. Like on your clock.

So, if you're household consumed five thousand kilowatts in the last hour, that means you used five kilowatt hours. That's how it works, for the most part. But the most important thing to remember here is—like most of the numbers on the pages of your electric bill—the lower, the better.

Base Charge

This is the amount the vampires at the electric company suck from your bank account even if you don't use *any* electricity.

"What?!?" you rightfully exclaim. Yeah, I know. It's total bullshit, but true none-the-less. Even if you were to go out of town tomorrow and stay gone for the rest of the month, chances are, your next electric bill will still not be zero. Now, not all plans use this kick-in-the-pants method of extracting money, but nearly half of the plans listed at Powertochoose.org, for instance, include a base charge. It may just be time for you to evaluate who your electric provider is—and whether vampires work there.

Current Charges

This one is easy, right? Not so fast. You might be thinking, "this is just the dollar equivalent of the Usage we talked about earlier," but you'd be wrong. Added to Usage, are an entire shitstorm of other charges, mostly in the form of taxes and fees. Current Charges takes the entire said shitstorm, and adds them all up for the current month, then spits out in an egregious number from hell. That's Current Charges.

Energy Charge

Here we are! Now we can see exactly how much you spent on electricity in the last billing cycle. This is what you *probably* thought Current Charges was—a simple formula of usage multiplied by rate. Finally, you got something right. Go get yourself another beverage to celebrate. We'll wait. Ready? Cool. So, the point here is, if you get your usage down, you get this number down, you get your electric bill down, and you get your blood pressure down. Easy-peasy.

Delivery Charge

"Delivery Charge!?!" you ask. "This isn't the fucking post-office! I don't have an electric delivery man coming once a month to flirt with my wife and zap my home full of light-juice." Easy there, buddy. We know how you feel, but like it or not, more than one company is ganging up on your monthly electric bill. You may have never thought about it—I know I hadn't—but all those poles and wires running up and down the streets most likely don't even belong to your electric company. That's right, they belong to a separate company that you *also* pay on your electric bill. Delivery charges can vary widely, so it's important to look at more than just usage rates when comparing electric companies.

One-Time Charges

These are basically just the electric company's sneaky way of passing on their own overhead expenses to you. Clearing out overgrown vegetation around some power lines? No problem! Just pass it on to the customer. Preparing the electrical delivery system for a hurricane? That's right! Pass it on to the customer. There are many examples of these One-Time Charges. They can come in a variety of different code-names, and there is pretty much nothing you can do about them. But, at least, now you know. I like to ask my provider in advance what one-time charges I should expect to see on my bill throughout the year. That way I can complain later to no avail, when I find out they lied to me again, and charged me for way more than they had indicated.

Non-Recurring Charges

"Wait. Doesn't "Non-Recurring" and "One-Time" kind of mean the same thing?" you ask. Now you're catching on. These are all just fake-ass terms made up by the electric company to justify taking your money. Well, not quite. Non-Recurring charges do differ slightly from One-Time charges in that the former might happen more than once, while the latter, is likely to happen only one time per yearly cycle. Neither are a consistent part of your monthly bill. Don't hear me wrong there. You'll consistently see both of these types of charged, they'll just be different each month. Non-Recurring Charges can be anything from early termination fees, disconnection notice fees, minimum usage fees to customer care call fees, and a whole lot more. Of these insidious crimes, I'd like to discuss minimum usage fees in a little more detail.

Minimum Usage Fee

This is a real shitty one. We're all just trying to save money so we can afford more beer and hockey, right? And everyone keeps telling us that we should use less electricity to save the environment, anyway. "So why in the name of Thomas Edison, is the electric company charging me *more* when I use *less*?"

do you ask? That's a very insightful question, my friend. And the answer is … greed. Pure. Unadulterated. Greed. The vampirical executives at the top of these companies want to make sure that even if everyone starts implementing great electricity saving practices, they'll still be able to afford that private yacht trip through the Lesser Antilles, each year. So, they hedge their bets with a Minimum Usage Fee. Greed!

Amount Due

Everything rolled into one, final, painful number: Usage Fees, Current Charges, One-Time, Recurring, I hate you, Die a painful death charges, even previous unpaid balances. All of these line-items (that's a fancy term for "we're charging you for this, too!") add up to Amount Due. It's kind of like bloodletting, only with money, and instead of dying a shriveled, maddened invalid, you die of contorted rage or alcohol poisoning.

Changes in Rates

Surprise! We made your electricity bill higher. Yup, that's pretty much what Changes in Rates are. According to the Public Utility Commission of Texas, a change in rate charge can refer to "Any change in the customer's rates or charges due to the variable rate feature of the Terms of Service contract." Oh, you mean you didn't read those seven-hundred pages of fine print when you signed on to your current electric provider? Well, I guess this is *your* fault then. Maybe you'll think about that next time and bring a pair of readers when you switch providers. You might way to bring some extra heart medication as well, 'cause they all look about the same level of ridiculous.

Other Taxes and Fees

"We need a more reliable electrical delivery system!" shouts your senator. "We need better disaster preparedness!" demands your local government official. "We'll make the electric company pay for it," they all promise. Well, guess what? They lied. You're paying for it. What sounded like a good idea at the time, and you may have even voted in favor of, ends up being just another line-item on your electric bill. And sometimes they don't even pay you the courtesy of breaking these out so you can understand what they are! It's like being slapped by an invisible hand, each month. Some of these fees include:

- **Advanced Metering Surcharge:** This is supposed to be a more advanced and efficient method of monitoring your monthly electric usage—so naturally, they charge you more for it.

- **Gross Receipts Tax Reimbursements:** This non-sensical name refers to the fee that the electric company (read: you) pays for operating in a town of less than one-thousand people. Makes perfect sense... Let's just make pass that all on to the poor people of this small town who are just struggling to get by and afford beer. Great idea!

- **PUC Assessment:** A fee to recover another fee for administering the Public Utility Regulatory Act of 1975. Here's how the conversation went. Government: Do this stuff. Electric Company: That's too expensive. Government: Do it anyway. Electric Company: OK. Then they charge you, and the government charges you on top to monitor the whole thing. Wait a minute ... 1975? Shouldn't that all be paid off by now?

- And many others...

Price to Compare

This has become a common addition to the monthly electric bill. It basically means, the cost to provide electricity without the other taxes and fees included. Presumably, so you can compare that cost to different electric companies and make an educated choice. But don't get your hopes up, because the Price to Compare is typically way less than the actual amount you pay ... which *does* include all those other taxes and fees. Again, fantastic logic from our wonderful overlords. Super helpful.

Hopefully this helps take a little bit of the mystery out of the monthly electric bill, and ultimately leads to you having more control over the factors therein. More likely, you'll just be more depressed, like me. Some things you just can't un-know. But *if* you're still with us, and not in a drunken stupor, crying on the floor, then have patience—it's time to start saving money!

Chapter 3: Divorce Your Electric Company

Electric companies wield an enormous amount of power over our monthly bills. But one entity has even more power. The government. You may be surprised to find out that most of what plagues you in those monthly electric bills is actually regulated by those bureaucrats sitting in Washington. Now, if you're lucky, you might find yourself sitting in one of the following states: California, Connecticut, Delaware, Illinois, Massachusetts, Maryland, Maine, Michigan, Montana, New Hampshire, New Jersey, New York, Ohia, Pennsilvania, Rhode Island, Texas, and the District of Columbia (Washington D.C.). What do these places have in common, and why would it be lucky for you to live in one of them, you ask? Deregulation. Now deregulation means a lot of things, but the most important thing to know about it is, it gives you choice.

Be sure to do a quick google search to make sure nothing has changed since we typed this up. www.electrickchoice.com is usually a good resource.

Living in a deregulated energy market allows you, the user, to decide which energy provider you want to purchase your energy from. This forces the different providers to compete, and that competition results in lower prices. Not only that, but prices tend to fluctuate more from season to season, allowing you to take advantage of our first tip.

Switch Electric Providers from Season to Season

Seriously! This is actually a thing. Some providers are cheaper than others from one season to the next based on how they compete with other providers in the market. All you have to do is go through the complete hassle of managing it every few months, and you'll be well on your way to saving. Good luck!

Switch during the Winter

Now it may seem counter-intuitive, but most electric companies have lower rates during the winter months. This is the perfect time to take advantage of a long-term contract if your provider offers them. If they don't, feel free to kick them to the curb. And remember to renegotiate every year. Much like your phone contract, plenty of other companies are often willing to step in at a moment's notice and take over if you're not satisfied.

Ask for Discounts

Yeah, Really! We first-world-country inhabitants tend to forget about this all-too-useful tool. But bartering can save you a lot of money, and sometimes all you have to do is ask. You might be surprised to find that some companies even expect to have to win your patronage with these types of giveaways and build them into their options. Now, they're not going to volunteer the information, so be sure to ask.

Ask for a Meter Upgrade

Believe it or not, the type of electric meter you have is the first step to more accurately monitoring your usage. And as we discussed in the last chapter, knowledge is power, and power is money. So, after you've asked them for some discounts, go ahead and ask them to come out to the property. You can bet they are not going to volunteer to give you an upgrade without a nudge, but they also don't want to lose you. Sometimes asking for a little can get you a lot.

Chapter 4: Your AC Filter is Dirty than My Internet Search History

Temperature Control

Now that your settled into the optimal energy provider (for those of you in deregulated areas) and paying the lowest rate possible for your electricity, we're going to show you how to use less of it. And there's no better place to start than the heating and cooling of your home. This simple element of comfort can regularly contribute up to fifty to sixty percent of your overall electric bill! But it doesn't have to, if you're willing to take a few easy (and a few not-so-easy) steps.

Adjust your Thermostat

We've already talked about how much energy your HVAC uses. It's a big, hungry, energy-sucking machine, and during the extremes of summer and winter it runs pretty much all the time. So, naturally—if you want to reduce the amount of money it's sucking out of your wallet—make the thing run less. Turn that temperature down in the winter, and up in the summer. All you have to worry about now is buying more blankets for you and your family, so you don't freeze to death in January. And the fact that you're now going to have to be changing the sheets every day in the summer... Hmm... Maybe this isn't a good one. Do it anyway!

Clean or replace your home's HVAC filter monthly

That's right, *monthly!* Maintaining your HVAC filter will keep that perfect, dust-free air circulating around your home like a fresh breeze. Studies show that this little bit of maintenance alone, can save up to 15% on your overall energy bill. You see, when all that hair from that cat or dog that you didn't want to buy your kids in the first place, gets clogged in the HVAC filter, the air has a harder time moving through it, which puts strain on the motor. One thing leads to another and *boom,* your electric bill goes way up. And that's just the best-case scenario. Too much strain on that motor over time can lead to much worse problems, like overheating, and in extreme cases, quitting on you altogether. Let me tell you from experience, HVAC repair is not a small invoice. So, it's best to just get rid of the cat and keep the filter clean and new. Now, those little filters *can* get pretty expensive themselves, so I recommend simply cleaning them rather than replacing for a couple of months. Then fully replace. Go ahead and set a calendar reminder so you don't forget. A good way to remember, is every time you pay your electric bill, it's time to replace your filter.

Weather-Stripping

No. This isn't about going outside in the rain and performing an erotic dance for your neighbors. You're such a pervert! This is about those gaps around your doors and windows that are letting out all that air you spent so much money conditioning. Don't believe me. Go ahead, walk over to your front door. Now get down real low and place your hand in front of the gap at the bottom. Feel that. If it's the middle of winter, you're probably feeling an icy draft. Maybe its summertime, though. In that case step outside, close the door and repeat. It's that nice cool inside air your feeling this time, isn't it? Worry not my frugal friend. With a little bit of weather-stripping, you can trap those unwanted breezes where they belong, *and* trap some more of your money in your checking account.

Ceiling Fans

Love to get blown? Why don't you already have ceiling fans? Seriously, how cheap are you? Listen, one of the best ways to run your air-conditioner less is to keep the air in your house moving, and that means ceiling fans in every room. That's right, every single room! You already know how to keep them spinning in the right direction from the previous chapters. And this doesn't just help in the summer. Keeping the air circulating around the house helps better use the warm air your heater or fireplace is already pumping out when it's cold outside, as well. So, get to the hardware store and snag a cart-full of their cheapest home-builder specials. They'll cost you dollars to purchase, and only pennies a day to run. You'll be saving in comfort in no time.

Programmable or Smart Thermostat

Again, how is this not already in your house. What are you even using to manage your HVAC? Well, don't be too embarrassed. Apparently not having one of these *is* a common enough thing, because it cracks pretty much every top-10 list on the Internet for things to buy to save energy. If you don't have one, get one. It's basically like your microwave; set it and forget it. Just program the temperatures you want to run during different times of the day/month/year and go sit back down in front of the TV with a beer. To be clear, I was not trying to rhyme here. Oh dear...

Inspect and fix those leaky HVAC ducts

"Woah! What? Who do you think I am, some handy-dandy tool-guy?!?" you shout angrily. Calm down, buddy. This isn't as hard as it sounds, and as long as you have access to your attic or basement—depending on whether you're a southerner or a yank—you should have no problem googling up some YouTube videos and DIYing this out of the park. The problem is a simple one. HVAC ducts can often have leaks. Sometimes they aren't installed particularly well in the first place. Maybe someone who owned your house before, (I know you would never do this), decided to cheap out and hire that guy that their cousin's friend knew that had done that work on their house before he went to jail. Maybe not. Sometimes the seals, where the ducts connect to each other or the vents, just come loose. In either case, the solution can often be as simple as some duct-tape. Do your own research on the proper method, and feel free to hire someone if you're as lazy as I am, but by all means, get those holes plugged, and stop air-conditioning your basement, crawlspace, or attic. Unless you have someone living in those spaces. I guess, then it's probably a good idea.

Don't leave the door open

You know what they say; "If you were a door, I'd slam you all night." This applies to the windows as well. Every time you open the door to your house, huge amounts of expensively conditioned air escapes out into the world, and all that unconditioned world-air comes back in to take its place. Then you have to spend all that money again conditioning this new world-air. Oi! Just keep it closed if you're not coming in or out, already.

Leave the door open

"Wait? But you said..." That's right, I did! And I'm not contradicting myself. At least that's what I tell my therapist... Seriously, the secret to this little trick is floating on the breeze. Sometimes when it's hot outside, there can still be a pretty good cross-breeze coming through. Open the right doors and windows, and you can harness the power of said breeze to cool your home without even running your AC. Just make sure you have proper screens installed, because summer usually equals bugs.

Make sure Air Vents are not Blocked

Often times, the air vents in our homes are positioned low on the wall or even in the floor itself. When this is the case, it can often happen that a dresser, rug or other piece-of-home-furnishing-that-you-didn't-want-to-replace-already-because-it-was-fine-in-the-first-place gets set on top of them, blocking the air flow, and causing havoc. Similar to having a plugged air-filter, blocking a vent causes the HVAC system to work extra hard, and can create some of the same, very expensive side-effects.

Window Coverings

You might already have these, but then again, you might not. If not, then you probably aren't married and/or don't care to be. I get it. I was single once. But finding a mate is not the only reason to have respectable looking windows. Another reason is—you guessed it—to save money. Covering your house's eyes to the world will help block all the light and UV that is constantly bombarding your interior spaces. Not only will this help your house stay cool and save energy, it will also keep your neighbors from having to see you do push-ups in your underwear every morning in your living room. You can't un-see that, so do your neighborhood a favor, and buy some drapes.

Move your Thermostat

This one was definitely new to me and made me think about making a change in my own home. Granted, the thought passed, and I still ended up on the couch doing nothing, but that's neither here nor there. The fact is, moving your thermostat might save you a lot of money. According to several online sources I trust very much—which for me is basically any online source—the best place to have your thermostat is on an interior wall that best replicates the normal temperature of your house at any given time. In other words; don't put it next to an air vent that is going to be blowing cold or hot air on it. Don't put it in the direct light of a window. Don't put it above your stove. Don't put it in your dryer—you know, that kind of thing. According to these same online sources, moving the thermostat to a proper location could help you maintain a better internal temperature without massive fluctuations. This will keep you and your

HVAC motor more comfortable and save you lots of green.

Say "No" to Santa

The fireplace is a wonderful thing, providing heat, ambiance, and nostalgia throughout the colder months. Another thing it provides if not used properly, is higher electricity bills. Having the chimney flue open when not in use lets in a lot of cold air, and then your house has to work extra hard to stay warm. So, say "no" to that red-garbed, toy-bringer this holiday season, and keep your chimney flue closed on Christmas Eve night. Enjoy the milk and cookies!

Reverse the Ceiling Fan

...unless it's already spinning the right direction, that is. Oh, you didn't know there were right and wrong directions for those blades to spin? Well, get ready to save. Here's the scoop. During the summer, there is a lot of hot air circulating around, and all of it ends up hanging around the ceiling. You're looking at me all glassy-eyed. Did you not know that hot air rises? Well it does. So make sure that the ceiling fan is spinning so that it's pulling air upward. This will send the hot air back down and then it will rise again. This cycle of fall and rise causes great circulation throughout your rooms, and helps the air feel cooler. During the winter you'll want to make sure the fan is blowing down, so all that hot air gets blown right towards you.

Turn Fans off when Not at Home

We already talked about how running your fans can save you money by keeping the internal temperature feeling cooler than it is. Now let's discuss why you shouldn't always keep them running. If you're away from home, and only your pets are still in the house, it's probably just fine to turn those fans off. Just keep the HVAC going at a crisp 78-80 degrees and they'll be fine. Alternatively, you could just get rid of the little money-suckers and be done with it, altogether.

Bundle up in the Winter

What is more romantic than digging deep into your closet for that arctic coat that you never use, and snuggling up on the couch with it for some much-anticipated show-binging? I mean, who doesn't like wearing seven layers inside the house? It feels a little like camping, only with all the conveniences of your modern home, right? So, dust off that goose-down jacket and gloves, and turn on the old ... crap, I can't quite click the ... buttons ... on this ... remote. Oh well. Just snuggle.

Turn HVAC off when Not at Home

This is just like the car, right? You go outside, turn it on, and the AC starts pumping. Turn it off and the AC turns off. Why *wouldn't* this work with your home? Just leave some bowls of ice-water sitting out for your pets and kids; they'll be fine. They're basically the same thing, anyway.

Install some Insulation

One thing that contributes a huge amount to the efficiency to a heating and cooling system is how well your house is insulated. And just like that top-notch beer cooler you just dropped four hundred dollars on, keeping your home at the optimal temperature can put you back a few bucks. But, from properly insulating your home's walls and floors, to simply wrapping your attic ladder in a bag (yes, that's really a thing) proper insulation is critical to long-term saving. One way to pinpoint where insulation can have the biggest impact in your home is to purchase a heat gun. These devices can help you find existing leaks, so you'll know exactly where to spend the most effective dollars. A couple of places that are often forgotten about are in the attic, and between your house and condenser unit.

Chapter 5: Are You a Washing Machine? Because I Want to Put a Full Load In You.

The Laundry Room

Your laundry room is a thief. It steals your time. It steals your socks—or at least one sock from each pair. And worst of all, it steals your money. In this chapter we'll be exploring strategies to make your washer and dryer less of the energy hungry machines they are. We may not be able to get your socks back, but we can help you save some money.

Run full Loads

Guys seem to get this instinctively ... or maybe it's just that they're lazy and don't want to wash their clothes until they absolutely run out, and then the only option is to stuff that washing machine until it cries. Either way, whether you're doing a load of laundry, or running a load of dishes, be sure to fill that machine up. Running full loads will reduce the amount of said loads you do throughout the month, and then, when that electric bill comes, you'll be dancing around in your freshly cleaned, overly worn underwear.

Wash Clothes on Cold

So much household energy is sucked right out through the washing machine, so that is where much can be saved. All you have to be willing to do is have dirty clothes all the time. Don't they say to wash your hands with hot water? Shouldn't the same apply to anything you wash? Whatever. Smell bad and save some money by washing your clothes on cold. Give it a try. These suggestions are getting ridiculous. I'm just throwing my hands up over here.

Air Dry your Clothes

Throw out that too-expensive, always-braking-down dryer. That thing takes up too much room in the house anyway. Rope, poles, and some outside air; that's all you need. Your neighbors are sure to find it charming, like an image out of an old movie, or that book you were supposed to read in middle-school but didn't and failed the class. No? Neighbors not finding it charming at all? Well, I do. And I'm certain you'll find it charming every time the electric bill comes. Just make sure you sit out on the porch and watch the clothes all day like a hawk. I'm just kidding. Nobody's going to steal your tattered-ass undies. Heh-heh ... ass undies. Plus, your clothes will last 10x times longer. The dryer heat destroys the clothes over time.

Empty the lint trap

What are you, five?! You should know this shit. Surely your mother scolded you time and time again when you were in college—and still living at home like a failure—for always forgetting to remove the lint from the dryer's lint trap after every load. That still hasn't sunk in? Well now is the time, because it's no longer your mom bitching at you, it's your bank account. Next time you dry a load of those fifty pairs of underwear that you should have thrown out five years ago, take the extra three seconds to scrape out the lint trap like an adult. Having a trap full of lint makes the dryer work much harder, and the harder it works, the harder it is going to be for you to stomach your electricity bill each month.

Use Dryer Balls

Not dryer, as in more dry, you disgusting ape. Dryer, as in the thing you dry your clothes in. Now that we've got that all sorted...

If you're like me, you're probably trying to figure out how to spend more money and take extra time every time you do a load of laundry. No? Well, too bad, because that's what this is all about. Actually, it's about saving money. Not much, but some. Using dryer balls is a good way to give your dryer that kick-start it needs to dry your clothes in less time, therefore using less energy. And some say it makes your clothes smell better, too. I don't know, because I'm a man, and the only things I can actually smell are barbecue and other people's farts.

Put Washer on the Shortest Cycle Possible

Your clothes aren't normally *that* dirty, dude. In fact, most times, we wash our clothes before they even need it. Have you heard of the smell test? Just a quick sniff can tell you a lot. It might tell you that the pants you're taking off belong back in the drawer rather than the hamper. But if they are ready to wash, remember that your machine probably has settings for a reason. Long cycles are only necessary for the most-soiled clothing—like after a day hiking, or a beer infused binger. If that hasn't been your day, chances are a quick cycle is all that is necessary.

Deep-clean the dryer

And after you scrape out the lint trap, here's a bonus task for you. Google, "how to deep clean my dryer." All that lint that was getting crammed harder and harder into the trap, because your ass was too lazy to remove it, has probably found its way out of said lint-trap and into all the internal workings of the machine itself. Make sure you unplug it first, and then get yourself up in there real nice and deep-like and get all that lint out. This will help your machine run easier and cost you less money on electricity. A note on safety: You should probably do your own safety research here—brush up on all things Current, Resistance and Conductivity. Yeah, that's going on pretty much all the time in these appliances, so unless you want to get dead quick, you'll want to make sure you aren't grabbing onto a wire that wants to make you its conductor. Another bonus to deep cleaning the dryer is the possibility of finding all those things you forgot to turn out of you pants pockets before washing them. It's a lot like when you turn over the couch cushions once a year and find enough coin for a free trip to the movies.

Clean the dryer vent

No, no. I'm not talking about the lint trap. We've already covered that—and you've already cleaned it out, right? This is that big tube that runs out the back of the dryer and probably punches through a wall or up to the roof. The dryer vent is responsible for expelling the hot air from the machine into the outside air, so it doesn't fill your laundry room up with the stuff. It also often contains some minor amounts of lint that the trap couldn't catch, or in your case, was too full to handle. These particles add up over time and end up making a mess of the inside of the vent tube, so make sure you either get all handy, or hire a professional to clean it our every six to twelve months. Your dryer will work better, and you'll save money.

Extra-Spin Cycle

"What?!? You want me to use the washing-machine *longer* in order to *save* electricity?" you ask. "That doesn't make sense sir!" I know. I thought the same thing, but bear with me for a moment. Imagine that your dryer uses way more electricity than your washing-machine. It kind of makes sense, right? I mean the dryer cord *is* much beefier than that regular-looking washer cord. Surely there must be more go-juice flowing through it. Now, further imagine that running an extra spin-cycle in the wash might get a lot more water out of your clothes than just the one spin, therefor allowing your dryer to dry said clothes much faster. Still not getting it? Just put those two imaginings together and what you have is a perfect world, wherein your dryer can dry your clothes up to twice as fast and use half as much energy. This saves way more energy on drying time than you are losing with the extra spin-cycle. Viola! Money saved

Switch to Gas

Do you have a gas water heater, or oven? Then you're in luck. Gas appliances often use energy more efficiently than their electric counterparts. Plus, fire is just way cooler than invisible magic juice. Well, maybe not. It doesn't matter, really. If you have access to gas and you're currently still rocking an old electric dryer, you should consider swapping that bad boy out for a fire burning equivalent. Chances are you'll save money and you'll feel more like a caveman while you're at it.

Get a Front-Loader

Have you ever seen one of those washing machines that looks kind of like a dryer? It has the glass door on the front and all. Next time you pass one as you're wasting time hiding from your wife in the hardware, stop for a moment and give the sales tag a quick read. These modern versions of the traditional top-load washing machine use way less water, and less electricity. The combination of those two factors means you'll save money over time. They're also just easier to use, since you don't have to reach all the way down into the tumbler to find that last sock. Just a hint—it isn't there. Say bye-bye to that pair.

Upgrade

Yup, it's time my penny-pinching friend. You've been hanging on to all those old appliances for so long, they don't even carry parts for them. Not only do newer washers and dryers use less energy, they also come with all kinds of cools features for your convenience. You won't be able to figure out how to use them, so you'll want to ask your technology kids to teach you about them.

Chapter 6: Save Power, Have Sex with the Lights Out

Confucius say, beauty is only a light switch away.
--Zen(ish) proverb

Let there be light

But not too much of it, and not the wrong kind, and not when you're not in the room. There are a lot of ways to lose electricity unnecessarily with that bringer of vision, and in this chapter we're going to teach you how to see and save.

Turn off the Lights during the day

This seems pretty obvious. The birds are chirping. The sun is out. Glorious light is pouring in through the windows. You're wasting another perfect day, binging TV on the couch. But for some reason, you still have every light turned on in the living room. Why? The sun is sitting up there in the sky like a huge free light-bulb. Open those curtains, and let it do its job. Then you can turn those lights off and enjoy the beauty of natural light! Don't care about natural lighting. Me either, but I like saving money.

Replace those Incandescents

You know those cheap light bulbs that you've always bought? The ones that come, one hundred to-a-pack, and you don't need a down-payment on or layaway program to afford. Yeah, those ones. Stop buying them. They don't last very long. They use a whole lot of energy, and they burn really hot compared to the newer offerings. Instead, opt for said newer offerings. There are a few different kinds to choose from. Halogens offer the best approximation of natural light and use a little less energy than the old Incandescents. Fluorescents are a bit cold in their glow, but light up big areas relatively easily, and use still less energy. CFLs use even less electricity and are commonly used as replacements in household applications. But LED bulbs take the cake when it comes to energy-efficiency. They also last the longest. Do your own research and see which one works the best for your goals and budget. This way, your crunchy-ass, environmentalist neighbor will finally stop rolling his eyes at you, *and* you can save some money in the process. Added bonus: you won't be changing them every month or unscrewing them and looking like a dumb ass shaking them next to your ears.

Motion Detectors

Remember last time you went to the bank to re-mortgage your house because you were out of money (because you were spending too much on electricity)? And when you stepped into the bathroom, the space went from dark to light just as you opened the door without you having to touch the switch? That's what we're talking about here. Motion detectors take all the inconvenience and guesswork out of turning lights off when you (and your teenage son) are not in the room. They work on a timer so that when you leave the room, they automatically turn the lights off after a few seconds. And, they have the added bonus of scaring the shit out of your friends the first time they come over and use the bathroom. Let's be honest; no one expects this kind of sophistication from you.

Dust your Bulbs

No. Not the ones in the garden. Those are supposed to be dirty. No! Not those ones. Get your mind out of the gutter. I'm talking about light bulbs. Over time, a significant amount of dust can build up on these light-producers, which can dramatically reduce their effectiveness. Dusting them regularly will keep them shining out like they are supposed to, and that will keep you from having to turn extra lights on just to keep from stumbling blind through your house. So, dust those bulbs once a month and save some money at the end of it.

Don't Over-light Rooms

According to some smart people, a lot of energy is wasted by pumping too much light into our living spaces. These same smart people have discovered that too much light can actually be bad for your eyes, as well. I mean, I guess that makes sense. It hurts when you stare into the sun, right? So, I guess, too many lightbulbs on in the same room could hurt your peepers the same way. So, what is the right amount of light, then? Apparently, there are whole websites dedicated to answering these questions, but the short answer is, it really depends on the purpose of the room. The amount of light needed is measure in something called "lumens," and a room like your living room needs way fewer of these per square feet as compared with an office space. So jump on the old google, figure out how many lumens you need, and get to optimizing. Before long, you'll be straining less and saving more.

Set the Mood

No, we're not talking about the romantic mood that your wife insists was there at the beginning of your relationship but disappeared with your college physique. We're talking about that money-saving mood. And to accomplish this, you're going to have to replace those old on-off switches on your wall with a better cost-saving version, called the "dimmer-switch." With these newer models installed, you'll be able to pretend to be creating a better ambiance for your wife, while smiling on the inside at the amount of money you'll be saving by using less light, and therefore less energy. She doesn't even need to know... She probably knows. You're not that sneaky.

Chapter 7: Did You Just Come Out of the oven? Because You're Hot.

Change the Temp in the Fridge

Much like the HVAC, turning the temperature up to the limits of your fortitude can help save energy. Who needs optimally cold foods, right? I know I like lumpy milk. Who doesn't? Room temperature beer? Uh, yes, please! A fellow can endure quite a bit to save a little money.

Clean out the Fridge

Your fridge is running non-stop all day, every day. And that's a good thing. It keeps your beer cold. But one of the most important aspects of keeping a consistent internal temperature is air flow. Your fridge circulates cold air throughout all of its spaces, and in return you have properly conditioned beverages. If your fridge is too full—read, packed full of leftover pizza boxes and Chinese takeout—it won't be able to circulate that air. Bad news bears! Throw out the garbage—and maybe run a wet rag over all the shelves in there while you're at it—and start saving energy.

Vacuum the Fridge Coils

Now that the fridge is all clean on the inside, let's take care of those coils on the outside. Have you ever even looked behind your refrigerator? Well, pull that big boy out from the wall, and take a peek. You'll probably see something that looks a bit like a grill grate smashed on the back. That is known as the coils, and that, my friend, is the key to keeping your seven-layer dip at the optimal temperature until game-day. The way it works is ... magic, snake-oil, hell, I don't know how it works. I just know that when those coils fill up with dust, and dog-hair, and toys your kids like to throw back there, over time, it stops working as well. So, get rid of your dog, and dust off those coils. Your dip will be a hit, and your wallet will be a little fuller.

Keep your oven clean

This is a similar concept to the HVAC filter. Basically, when all that cheese from the pizza you eat every night builds up all over the heating coils in the bottom of the oven, it makes the poor appliance have to work even harder to get up to the proper cooking temperature. And the harder it has to work, the more money it burns in the process. It also makes it more difficult to get that perfect, golden-brown crust on the pizza, which is by far the worse of the two problems. So, fix your dinner *and* your wallet by making a point to regularly clean out your oven. Sound hard? Don't worry, most ovens even have an automatic cleaning function, so your lazy ass has no excuses.

Turn the Burner off a Little Early

Ok, so the rest of the tips in this chapter are actually pretty cool and may be new to you. I had certainly never heard of this one. Next time you're cooking on the stovetop—and your eggs are beginning to look a lot like something dead you saw in the road on the way home last night—go ahead and turn that burner off. Better-yet, turn it off before the eggs are burnt. Better, better yet, cut the heat before they're even done cooking. The pan will stay hot—Yeah, newsflash—and continue to cook the eggs. This may take some practice, and your uncoordinated Neanderthal brain may never pick it up fully, but the good news is, you won't use as much electricity on burner time you don't need in the first place.

Toaster Over

This is basically like a tiny oven. Like a little, toy version of the huge machine you have taking up three feet of wall space in your crowded kitchen. Imagine a microwave, only instead of slowly making you sterile with radiation, this thing just uses electricity and heat. It's actually pretty convenient. Essentially, instead of heating up the entire cavernous inside of your giant oven each time you want to re-heat yesterday's last slice of pizza, you can use this smaller version to do the same job, in less time, and using less energy.

Scrape those Plates

Kids didn't finish that homemade, vegan lasagna your wife invented? Yeah, I don't blame them either. What is tofu, really? Seems untrustworthy... Anyway, make sure you scrape those plates in the trash before you rinse them. This simple act will keep unnecessary solids out of the garbage disposal, and out of the dishwasher, allowing both to run smoother, faster, longer, and save you electricity in the process.

Cover Pots with Pans

If you're boiling water, covering the pot with a corresponding sized pan will help keep that heat in said water, and bring it to boil quicker, and using less energy. An added bonus to this technique that you'll never use, is once your water is boiling, you can remove the pan and use it immediately to cook something else; it will already be hot. What's that? No. The pot is the deep one. The pan is the flat one. Sheesh!

Move the Fridge

This is pretty much the same concept as the thermostat. Your fridge is supposed to stay cold, right? So, keeping it in the direct light of a south-facing window is probably a bad idea. It will have a harder time maintaining that perfect temperature and use more electricity. Move that behemoth to another, shadier location. Perhaps another wall in the kitchen. Perhaps the basement next to your deadbeat brother's cot. Either way, move it and save some money. And talk to your brother while your down there. He misses you, and he's beginning to have conversations with the rats.

Thaw your Food

This is just good practice anyway. You can't really call yourself a bonafide grill-master unless you're thawing those choice cuts before throwing them on the heat, right? Well, now you have an added incentive to properly prepare your meat; it saves you money. Thawing your food, makes it easier and less time-consuming to cook, and that means, less power used. So when your friend are all complaining because they're hungry and the game is about to start, you can smile knowing that all that extra time spent waiting means better food, and money saved.

Use Tiny Cooking Tools

What if I told you, there is actually a reason that the pot-and-pan set you finally agreed to purchase came with sixty-four different pieces? You're going to want to sit down. Sitting? Good. Because, there is. And it's all about saving energy. *And* about cooking properly, I suppose, but mostly saving money. You see, when you use the right size pot, for instance, to boil up some spaghetti, that means you're also using the right amount of water. Using the right amount of water means you aren't heating up more water than you need to. And not heating up excess water means you aren't using excess energy. You see

where I'm going with this now? Fantastic.
Now stop pretending you knew that spaghetti
was boiled.

Air-Dry your Dishes

It doesn't just work with clothes, folks.
Air drying is a good idea for pretty much
anything you need to dry. I'm sure your guests
won't mind all those water-spotted dishes.
And if they do, should you really be hanging
out with those kinds of people, anyway? While
you're at it, why don't you just start air-drying
yourself. The evaporative cooling effect should
keep you cool on those AC-less summer days.
Bonus!

Heat your Water Before You Heat your Water

Bear with me, I'm not crazy. The magic
here is in the relative difference in efficiency
between your stovetop and the microwave. It

is actually more energy efficient to heat up water in the microwave, and then bring it the rest of the way to boil on your electric stovetop, then it is to boil all the way from cold on the stove. It might be a little more inconvenient, sure, but isn't all that extra money worth a few extra steps?

Ditch the Extra Fridge

You remember when you got that huge deep-freeze back in the 80's with the intention of filling it up with deer-meat that you were going to learn how to hunt, but then you never went hunting and ended up filling it up with ice-cream, which you've never eaten (also from the 80's)? Get rid of it. It's just sitting there sucking away your retirement. Donate it, or scrap it, or take it outside and practice shooting at it. I don't care what you do, just make sure it isn't plugged in to your wall anymore.

Fill That Dishwasher Up

Just like the washer and dryer, your dishwasher uses a ton of energy every time it runs. Filling it up as much as possible allows you to run it fewer times and saves you money. Plus, this method allows you to rely on that most human of strategies, which you've perfected since you were in grade-school—procrastination. Embrace your lazy self, and stuff that dishwasher to the brim.

Unplug Things When Not in Use

You're done with the toaster oven? Unplug it. Finished zapping water in the microwave? Disconnect it. Never use that too-expensive juicer. Just throw that thing away. So, the time is always wrong on your appliances. Who cares? That's what your smart-phone is for, right? So use the appliances for appliance-ing and your phone for telling time. Unplug those energy suckers when you're not using them and save some money.

Chapter 8: Save Water, Shower Together

Save Water, Save Money

"Hold on! I thought this book was about saving money by using less *electricity*. Now you want to talk to me about water? What gives?!" you ask, astutely. That's right, my greedy friend; reducing water waste not only has the benefit of saving you money on your water bill but can save you a ton on your electricity bill as well. The reason? We really like hot water, and unless you're rocking a gas water heater, then your hot water is a result of the electrical grid. Let's take a look at several ways to leave a little more of that electricity in the grid where it belongs.

Turn your Water-Heater Down

Yeah. No problem. Just take cold showers every day. You'll probably be craving some cold showers in the summer based on some of the tips in this book. Just find your water-heater (it's usually in the basement, a small closet, or the attic), turn that heat knob down, and prepare for some shrunken uhm ... parts. And if you remember the tip about running the washing-machine on cold. There you go—two birds, one stone. You'll still kill all the bacteria you need and save some money. For the real adventurous folks, just turn it off completely.

Take Shorter Showers

See, I'm thinking *shorter* showers is just the *first* step. If shorter showers are better, surely, *no* showers are best! I say we boycott the entire showering experience. It's really a modern invention anyway, right? Let's do this! If we can get enough people on board, we can forget this whole shower-time/money-wasting experience ever existed in the first place. Or, I guess we could just take shorter ones. Whichever one, really. Your call.

Shower together

Still taking showers. I get it. They can be pretty pleasant. But if you're determined to keep enjoying this modern convenience at least share the experience. Invite your partner or really, really close friend to join you. You'll use less water and have a bonding experience at the same time. Win, win.

Fix your leaky faucets

Even a tiny leak allowed to run for long periods of time can add up to a lot of water, and if it's your hot water line that's leaking and you have an electric water-heater, then you are also leaking money on your electric bill. Every drop of hot water that escapes your faucet, is another drop that your water-heater has to replace and re-heat, ergo; using more electricity. So again, jump on the YouTubes, or hire a helping hand, and get those leaks fixed.

Turn the Water off, while Shaving

...or brushing, or washing the dishes by hand, or ... whatever doesn't require you to use water non-stop. Remember our little talk about leaky faucets earlier and how they can actually add significantly to your electricity bill. Yeah, that's what this is all about. Having the water running while you meticulously shave every last hair from your face, is like having a leaky faucet times one-hundred. So, turn that water off between strokes. Just a simple little behavioral adjustment here can save you some serious moolah. And while you're at it, just get rid of those electric bathroom appliances. Your electric razor is just a death trap, and that electric toothbrush? Wasteful. Stop being lazy and use those arms!

Low-flow Fixtures

I feel like we've discussed faucets way too much already. But by God, I'll be damned if there isn't yet another way to save some electricity at the sink. Add to that, the toilet and the shower for this installment. That's right, replace basically anything that emits water in your house with a low-flow version of itself. Who cares that you'll never get all that soap off your hands our out of your hair. I mean, maybe your wife, kids, friends, and boss will care, but that's beside the point. And never-mind that your toilet is probably going to back up every few weeks. You'll be so happy with your new, reduced electric bill, that you

won't even mind all the additional plunging.
Bonus! You'll also see a dent in your monthly
water bill.

Chapter 9: Is Your Name WiFI? Because I'm really Feeling a Connection.

Home Electronics

Hold on. Calm down. I'm on your side. I'm not about to tell you to get rid of all those precious devices that occupy 99% of your mental energy and 100% of your heart. I have them too. We all do, and we all love them. But … they *do* use a lot of electricity. So let's make your relationship with those bringers of entertainment ever better and spend less on energy in the process.

Ditch the Desktop; Buy a Laptop

Why do you even have a desktop computer? Is it glued to the top of the desk that it sits on by coke residue, and you just can't get it off to throw it away? Seriously, unless you are a hard-core gamer, or in the creative arts industry, you would probably be able to do anything you ever needed to on a simple, thin, energy-frugal laptop. Another great reason to make the change is portability. You'll be able to haul this new information device with you to that doubles date you finally gave into, allowing you to keep streaming the game. Make the switch, watch the game, and save some money.

New TV

You already did this, right? Yeah, that's what I thought. TV is the only thing you truly care about in your life, so you get a new one every year just to make sure you're watching those dragons destroy those towns in the highest, smoothest definition possible. Well, good. And for the few of you out there who haven't replaced that old tube with a sweet new flat-screen—Shame! Seriously, it has never been easier than now to make the change. Prices are cheap, and you can find them everywhere. Hell, you don't even need to leave the couch. Just search up your favorite electronics store on your phone and order it. You might even get free delivery, and when it arrives you can watch with additional smugness as you save more money.

Smart Speaker

You know what I'm talking about. And the speakers do too...because they're that smart. There are only about a million smart-speaker options these days, and the great thing about these artificial intelligent companions is that they can manage all your smart devices for you. You can program them to run devices in your house on certain schedules, or give them commands in real-time, like "Turn the kitchen lights off," or "turn the AC on 'away' mode," or "cut power to my son's room." Options are practically endless.

Unplug Electronics when Not in Use

We talked about this earlier. Just because the power switch is turned to "off" doesn't mean those devices aren't still using electricity. So, remember to unplug that shit when you're not using it. The show's over? Unplug the TV. Done sending that text? Hard off. In fact, a great way to do this is to put all those appliances on power strips so you can just unplug on wire and watch them all go to sleep.

Remember those Power-Strips

Now that you've untangled that stacked mess of power-strip nightmare around your entertainment center, let's go ahead and throw those old, dust-covered, fire-hazards away. New versions are not only more energy efficient, but also help you monitor the energy your using. You might think turning off your TV or gaming box causes them to stop sucking energy out of the wall, but in most cases you'd be wrong. Most of these devices have what's called a standby mode, which actually keeps them turned on even when they appear off, so that they can pop into action quickly next time you want to shoot some baddies in that first-person-shooter you can't get past the first level on. This uses lots of energy and using a power-strip that monitors energy usage can show you just which of those devices is robbing you blind. With knowledge, comes power. No, not the power you need to get past the first level. This is the power to save money.

Stop Using the Treadmill

Treadmills actually use a pretty decent amount of electricity, believe it or not. So why not take your sneakers to the pavement or a trail and get some fresh air while you're burning those calories. Your spirit will be better for it or some shit like that, *and*, your electric bill will get slimmer as well. Win-win. I'm just kidding. I know you don't own a treadmill.

Play a Board Game

You remember Monopoly, right? That multi-day fight-fest that you swore you'd never play again with your family three Thanksgivings ago? You've all grown since then, right? Maybe it's time to dust off the old dice and give it another go. Even if you do argue the whole time, at least you won't have to worry about it using electricity. Just make your kids turn their phones off, first. Better yet, just grab a 5,000-word puzzle. That'd probably be easier.

Chapter 10: Do it in the Great Outdoors

Or Just Right Outside

Inside the home, isn't the only place you're wasting electricity. Lots of the stuff is used outside those walls, and you may not even realize it. But from lighting to landscape, there are tons of ways to reduce the use, and save some money.

Plant some Trees

Trees are wonderful things. You can hang a swing from them. You can build a treehouse in them. They look great. You can spy on your neighbor's wife from them. What? I've heard about ... other ... people doing that. Ahem... But among the benefits of trees, one stands tall above the rest—they can save you money. Trees are like nature's air-conditioners. Some studies show that properly planted trees can reduce your summer air-conditioning usage by up to a whopping 35%. That's a ton! So do the world a favor and plant some trees. Or just do it for the money. We're happy with either. Just make sure you don't plant them too close to the condenser unit. You want to make sure you're casting shade on it, but still allowing it to breathe.

Variable Speed Motor

If you haven't filled in your pool yet, then you're probably still spending a ton of money on its maintenance. One way to reduce the hurt, is to change out that loud clunky fixed-speed pump motor for a newer variable speed entry. Variable speed motors adjust their output based on what the demand is, so if there are a ton of people in the pool, it'll ramp up to handle it. And if all is calm, it'll adjust to that too. In the process, they use less energy. They're a lot quieter, too, so if you're determined to keep that backyard bathtub, maybe it's time to upgrade its engine.

Motion Sensor Lights

Not only are they super cool, motion activated lights also save you money. They stay off all the time when not needed and only spring into use when someone approaches. This is very handy for you and your family when coming home late from the recital you didn't want to attend and has the added benefit of scaring would-be thieves away.

Solar Lights

Another great money-saving lighting option is solar. Commonly used in path-lighting, these alternatives run on the sun, and never have to be connected to the grid. More and more options are hitting the market every day, so the time is now to make the investment, so you can save big over time.

Manual Yard-Maintenance Tools

Have you ever seen an old movie from the turn of the century back we used manpower, and horse-power, and not so much electric power and gas power? Looks pretty inconvenient, right? Those back broken laborers pushing those reel mowers. Those manual edgers and hedge trimmers. Well, maybe not so inconvenient. When you consider that those power-it-yourself tools don't use any electricity and double as a workout, you might just find yourself saving both time and money. They don't cost nearly as much to purchase either.

Chapter 11: New Skin for the Win

Giving Your House Some New Clothes

It's not quite outside, and not quite inside. It's that area in between—the walls, the windows, and doors. It's like your skin. And like your skin, taking care of it, will take care of your home. Not taking are of it, can cost you a lot on electricity. Let's take a look at several ways giving your home a new wardrobe can reduce your energy bill.

Upgrade your HVAC

This one can get a bit pricey, but in the long run, will be well worth it in savings and comfort. Be sure to pay attention to the SEER rating when selecting a new system. This is the efficiency rating of the system and is expressed as a numerical value ranging from thirteen at the worst, to twenty-five at the most efficient. Many companies claim that a high SEER rated system can pay itself off in savings many times over during its life. And, depending on how you finance it, it may save enough each month to offset the payments. But, probably not. Nothing in life is that convenient, right?

Install Double-Pane Windows

Still rocking those home-builder windows from the eighties? I get it. Windows are expensive, and why should you fix something that isn't broken, right? Well, they might be. No, don't jump up and go looking for cracks, I'm not talking about that kind of broken. I'm talking about the wasting a lot of energy kind of broken. Turns out those old windows aren't very efficient and replacing them with some double-pane alternatives can save you a lot.

Have Your Attic Audited

Didn't know that was a thing? Me either. Thanks, google! But now that you do, pick up the phone and ring up an auditor. They'll check to see how efficient your attic is at helping your home regulate temperature and make recommendations on how to make it better. This might mean installing more soffits, an electric roof fan for better air flow, better insulation, spray heat coating in the rafters, even simply covering the attic ladder with a thermal bag. All these can add up to a lot of cost up-front, but can also spell big savings over time.

Replace your Roof

Have you ever worn a black shirt on a hot day? Did you feel like the sun was pointed directly at your soul? That's because dark materials absorb more sunlight and heat than light-colored ones. This is particularly useful knowledge when thinking about replacing that beyond-its-useful-life roof of yours. Now you might be asking, "If darker colors absorb more heat, then why are so many roofs covered in a material that looks like a black asphalt road?" Good question. The answer is, those roofs are cheap... The cheapest, in fact. But they also put way more heat into your home, causing your HVAC to work way harder in the warmer months. They also don't last nearly as long as some of the more light-deflective alternatives. So maybe skip installing that pool this spring, and replace your roof with a nice light-colored, corrugated metal. If maintained properly (see previous chapters) It will last a lifetime, and help you save energy.

Install Solar Panels

Not quite ready for the whole wind-farm experience? That's ok, I've got a slightly less land and money intensive way for you to save on electricity. Not that it's cheap though—

solar panels cost a pretty penny or two themselves. Sometimes, however, the government is willing to help you with that part. Yes, that government. The same one that forces you to pay taxes on the money you earn, *even though* your employer already paid taxes on that same money when *they* earned it. The same one. All the more incentive to stick it to them, right? Go ahead. Apply for that government solar incentive program and start saving money on the back of greedy-old Uncle Sam.

Chapter 12: Kids Need to Earn Their Keep

They'll Love It

What kid doesn't want to spend some quality time with their dear-old parents? And what better topic than saving money on the electricity bill? Seriously though, you probably shouldn't bring that up unless you want to spend the entire time arguing. Try to set the tone as more of an opportunity to make memories that will last them a lifetime. Oh, they don't want memories of you? That's OK. Just force them to participate like everything else they're supposed to be doing on their own.

Have Disconnected Time

They say, "A family that plays together, stays together." Well, if playing means camping out on the couch, slaying hordes of the undead on the latest game-box, then you might be slaying your bank account at the same time. Not only do those games cost way too much in the first place, they also draw a lot of power from the grid. Is family really worth all that? Really? Well if you're still not ready to ditch the ties that bind, then perhaps consider some electricity free alternatives, such as board games, family reading sessions, or maybe even just talk. These "Disconnected Times" may just save your family and your wallet.

Keep the kids safe

Tired of your too-old-for-this-shit son asking you to come into his room every night to make sure there are no monsters under the bed? Tired of his continual requests to keep a light on in the closet or hallway, because, electricity ain't cheap? How about killing two ogres with one power-saving device? Get that little mamma's boy a shake-to-charge flashlight, so they can ward off the demons without warding away your savings. Make it an LED if you want to save some serious energy.

Watch TV Together

I know. This is a tough one. You're not into that anime crap your daughter like, not are you thrilled with the latest offerings from the romantic comedy section your wife keeps insisting you watch together. But, grouping up with your family for movie night *can* reduce the number of devices simultaneously being used by a significant number. And that comes with a lot of savings. Worth it? Ok. Just remember to make sure that all those other energy hogs are unplugged and not just turned off. With this new tradition, your kids will get to spend a little more time with dear-old-dad, *and* you'll get to inculcate them with all those movies from the 80's and 90's that you used to rot your brain with when you were their age. Can't you just hear them saying, "Thanks Dad for this wonderful time spent together. I don't at all miss playing video games in my room with my online friends." No? Good. Life's not fair. It's time they learned.

Solar Backpacks

Is your kid getting picked on at school for not being cool enough? We've got them covered. Nothing is cooler than a backpack that can charge all those devices he is too young to have and shouldn't be carrying around at school in the first place. But that's neither here nor there. A little time in the sun, and all his new friends will be flocking around him asking for a charge. Actually, maybe that isn't such a good idea. Those friends might want to come over and play on his gaming devices. Peace and quiet could be at stake. Best to keep the solar backpack for yourself.

Upgrade their Fish-tank

Tired of hearing that awful humming noise all day in the corner of the living room— that filtration system in your kids fish-tank that you didn't want in the first place, and now you spend way too much time keeping the cat (which you also did not want) out of. Well, I've got some good news for you. They make new, energy efficient filtration system. Many versions can be set so they don't run all the time and use less energy when they do. Just make sure you calibrate it correctly to your kid's fish's needs, or you may find yourself having to explain why Mr. Bubbles likes to swim upside-down all of the sudden. For bonus energy savings, switch out the tank's light bulbs for some newer LED models.

Take them Holiday Shopping

No, not for toys. You are still obligated to surprise them with those. I'm talking decorations, specifically lighting. I know, you've been hanging on to that set of lights you got when you first bought the house three re-mortgages ago, and you hate buying new stuff, but those Christmas mood-setters just might be sucking the energy out of your holiday fund. Take the kids with you for a trip to the hardware store, and stock up on LED Christmas lights. They last longer, glow brighter, and use way less electricity. While you're at it, put those lights on a timer so they're off during the day and after a certain hour of the night. Ho, Ho, Ho!

Take a Hike

Hide your kid's electronic devices, and head for the good-old outdoors. Maybe you have a favorite place your parents used to take you. Maybe you'd rather not think about your childhood. Either way, spending some time in nature, whether for a short walk or for a camping is a great way to spend some family-time, while giving your home energy system a break. Just remember to use all the gadgets you bought to make sure that your home is truly "off" before you go. And, watch for bears.

Dark Activities

Ever play hide-and-go-seek in the dark when you were a kid? We played it all the time. Kids love that shit. *And* they love playing with you. Give them what they want. Turn those lights off all day, and pretend it's because you're playing a great game of find'em, then just don't go looking for them. They'll think they are the best hider of all time, you'll save money, and you won't have to listen to your kids fighting all the time. Just make sure you yell out, "Where are you?"

about once every five minutes, or they might get suspicious.

Chapter 13: My Fetish is making the Electric Company Cry

Go Big or Go Home!

The author of the following content makes no claim that the suggestions herein are in any way respectable, moral, ethical, legal, and/or safe—only that if pulled off properly, they just might save you some serious money on your electric bill. Plug your nose, finish your will, get some extra life-insurance, and dive in! These are the extreme ways to save!

Move Your Life

I guess this one isn't so bad, I mean people move all the time. Most of them don't do it just to save money on electricity, but hey, to each their own. A newer house or apartment can help you save tons on electricity. They typically have many of the updated appliances and other feature we've already discussed, and often have the added benefit of introducing you and your family to a new neighborhood. Or no neighborhood—maybe just move out into the woods. Whatever your boat, get out there and float a newer one.

Get some Roommates

Know a few people who might want to bunk up and save some dough? No? Well... have you heard of Craigslist? People are everywhere, and one thing they all have in common? A desire to save money. However you find them, sharing utility costs can end up saving you a lot. Not to mention, more people to watch TV with, play games with, share that one shower ... with. Actually, this may not be a great option. But it *is* an option.

Turn Your Circuits Off at Night

Here's a really simple one with some big impacts. Head over to your circuit breaker. It's that big panel in the wall that has been mislabeled a billion times by families that lived in your house before you. Now figure out which circuit your fridge is on. Got it? Great, now when you go to bed at night, turn every other circuit off. Guess what, they won't be using any more power until you wake them back up. Just make sure you charge your phone during the day, so you'll still have an alarm clock in the morning.

Become Amish

You've seen those quaint buggies rumbling down the road. You've coveted those monochromatic clothes they wear. You've always wanted to know why these people never emerged from their colonial values. Heck, you've even wondered if a simpler life might be something *you*'d enjoy! Well, now you have just the inspiration you need. These motorless-magnates are the Kings and Queens of saving electricity. In fact, they save all of it. That's right. They use zero electricity. Does that sound good to you? Well then, ditch your razor and lather up your milking hands. It's time to break Amish!

Don't use the Oven in the Summer

I don't know. I don't know about this one guys. I mean, I guess I could do to eat a few more salads, but no pizza? No pizza for the entire summer? Holy shit! I think I'll just pay the bill. You try it if you want. I'm just paying.

Frost all of Your Windows

Most people are familiar with frosted glass. Many bathroom windows are made with the stuff. Maybe even some of yours. But did you know that frosted glass is not only for blocking the view of your pervert neighbor? It also blocks out heat. So, if frosting one window is good, then frosting them all must be better, right? Head on over to the hardware store and get yourself a kit. Join me and just say "no" to the sun.

Invest in Candles

Candles can be a great, inexpensive way to save on electricity. In case you're single, candles are those waxy things with the string sticking out the top. You light the string and they produce a small fire, perfect for lighting a tiny area of the dark. Place enough of them around you and you won't have to use electric lights at all. Depending on how you arrange them, you may also be able to communicate with dead relatives ... so... Free entertainment! They're pretty cheap these days, so now you have now excuse not to flicker up the house with savings and late Uncle Elroy!

Cook Outside Only

No, not just during the backyard barbecue. Not just the day you replace that previous grill that you bought, used once, then forgot about to time and rust. Every. Time. For. Ever. Or just when you want to. It's really up to you. What do I care? But if you do start cooking with the birds and the squirrels, you'll enjoy the advantage of not filling your house up with heat, and therefore forcing your AC to work overtime to cool it back down. That's all.

Cook Using a Solar Oven

Ever seen a solar oven. Me either, but I'm told they exist, and that they run on the sun's rays. The sun's fucking rays! You don't even have to pay for the sun's rays. It just gives them to us. For free. Every day. How much does a solar oven cost? I'm getting one. I'll finish this section later. The sun's fucking rays!

Drain the Pool

You go out there every single day. You skim the leaves off the top. You manage the chemicals just right. You keep it perfectly clear, and at just the right temperature. It's your pride and joy, and … then no one uses it. Your kids? They're too busy playing some stupid video game about stacking blocks on blocks to swim!?! Damn right they are. That game is the shit! But you know what they aren't too busy to do? Skateboard. Next summer, instead of spending those ten-plus hours a week keeping the pool just perfect, hang up that scoop, my friend. Drain that pool and viola, you've got yourself a backyard skate-park. And guess what? That skate-park; it doesn't require temperature control. It doesn't need fancy chemicals. It doesn't need a motorized circulation and filtration system. It only needs to be dry. Now I know what you're thinking. Don't do it. Seriously, don't try to skateboard with your kids. You'll just end up hurting yourself, or them. Just watch from the side, old man.

Stop Growing Drugs in your House

So, it was *you* and not your teenage son, cooking up that stinky weed? Well, props for the entrepreneurship. But what if I told you that habit might be contributing massively to your energy bill? Oh, you wouldn't care? Huh. Not how I thought that was going to go. How about if I told you that you could still get that good stuff, *and* avoid the massive heat drain? Now you're in? That's better, and the solution in simple. All you have to do is move to a state where the stuff is legal and buy it. Great, right? I'll help you pack. When are we leaving?

Lose the Pets

Yeah, yeah, I know, you'll have to listen to weeks of crying form your kids, because they love their iguana, and they just figured out how to keep it from biting them every time they try to pet it, and blah, blah, blah. But that's a small sacrifice to pay for more money, really, isn't it? Pets drain a ton of energy. That iguana probably has a heat lamp running 24/7 in its little cage of terror, right. Trust me, get rid of it now before they get even more attached and you'll be glad you did. Maybe, just get it stuffed. That sounds like a great dad-move, right?

Lose the kids and family

She guilted you into having the kids, anyway, right? Come to think of it, she probably guilted you into marriage too. Well, she probably knows she has this coming then.

Just be sure to use to reverse psychology, so she thinks it was actually her idea. Talk about how you just can't stand holding her back anymore, and how you don't want to see the kids turn out like you—you know, that stuff. Then hang your head until you're out of sight. One you're around the corner, you can start skipping all the way to the bank.

Install a Windmill

Have an extra acre of land and an extra cool $Mil laying around in your bank account? Fantastic! You're ready to start your very own, personal windfarm. You've always admired those sleek, handsome turbines turning in the distance as you drive home from your hell-job each day, right? Well now you can come home to one. And the greatest thing is, you'll never have to pay for electricity again—as long as the wind keeps blowing, that is. You might even be able to sell a little zap-juice back into the grid and take that extra holiday you've always wanted. Wait. You have an extra million dollars in your bank-account, and you aren't taking holidays. Nice saving, dude!

Hook Your Bike up to Your TV

Ok, not really. Well, sort of. I'm not talking about that bike hanging in your garage that you had all those aspirations of using every weekend to "unwind" but never did. I'm talking about a *special* bike. A bike that doesn't go anywhere and comes with a cord. When you get on said bike and start peddling, magic comes out of its ass, and shoots right into your home's electrical system. Seriously, this *is* a thing. Look it up. Then buy it. Then put it next to your other bike when you get tired of using it after the first week.

Steal

Yes, that kind of steal. Remember the clause at the top? I'm not telling you to do this—only that it *can* be done ... hypothetically. So ... hypothetically ... if one *was* to do this, they would need to be pretty handy with electrical systems. They would ... hypothetically ... wait until they knew their neighbor was going to be out of town, run some heavy cable over to said neighbor's house, do some electrical magicking to bypass a few of their own circuits, and *kazing!* Free electricity. Well, free for you. Your neighbor is probably going to get a shock at the end of the month. On second thought, if you're that handy with electrical systems, why are you even reading this book?

Leave the Grid Behind

You don't have to be Amish to stop relying on electricity, right? I mean, this is pretty much how we lived for like, hundreds of thousands of years—hunt, gather, wheel, fire, etc.? You just need to get back to your roots. Besides an addiction to TV streaming and smart-phone games where we mindlessly explode candy, what's stopping you? Kids? Bring 'em with? They like camping, right? Just tell them you're heading out for a stay in the old outdoors with dear-old dad, and then sell the house while you're out. They'll forgive you ... eventually.

Use Someone Else's Grid

This is a slight variation on "Steal," above, only this time, we're not siphoning energy back to our house—we're moving our asses right in. We're just not going to tell them about it. Haven't you seen that viral video circulating around the inter-webs—the one where the lady who lives alone keeps running out of food and knows she isn't eating it all, then sets up a camera and catches the perpetrator creeping out of her air vent at night. No, that isn't what I'm talking about. You'd be in the attic, not in the air vent. And you wouldn't get caught. That's what I'm talking about. Play your cards right, and *boom!* Free electricity, and free food when your new "host-mom" is at work.

Work the "Night-Janitor" Shift

Keeping with the theme here, in this take of stealing someone's else's electricity, we're going to actually move into a school, or museum—or anywhere that needs night cleaning and security services and has at least a sink for you to clean up in. Simply get rid of everything you own except for a few bare essentials and take showers while you're alone on duty. They will literally be paying you to use their electricity.

Get an Electric Car

...and live in it. It can't be that hard, right? I guess you'd have to have a pretty cush job to afford it ... and all that eating out you'd have to do every day, but hey, most cities have free charging stations now, so score! No electric bill. No mortgage. Another win-win for frugal McGee over here.

Make Your Own AC Unit

Trust me, you don't have to be MacGyver to cool your house, DIY-style. All you need is a will to save, a bucket, a fan, and a few hours of focused time. There are numerous videos floating around the webs to show you how to accomplish this feat, but the summarized version is this: 1) Put a bunch of ice in the bucket. 2) Point a fan so that it blows over said bucket full of ice. That's it. The air will interact with the ice in a phenomenon called evaporative cooling, and soon, you'll be kicking back in comfort and savings.

Stop Eating

Much of the energy you use every month goes directly into your stove, oven, microwave, toaster, blender, mouth, etc. etc. etc. What do all these things have in common? They are all related to you eating food. "Wait a minute, you don't mean to say that I should stop eating altogether, right? You mean just stop eating certain foods like my wife is always trying to get me to do, right? Right!?!" No, sir. I mean all of it. There's a new wave in healthy eating these days, (this is actually true) wherein you live on water and the sun's energy, alone. That's it. No one has proven yet that it actually works, of course, but hey, those people must be using way less electricity.

Stop Bathing

By now, you know that hot water is a major energy user. You also know that bathing is a major user of hot water. So basically, I'm giving you a choice here. Either bath in cold water; who the hell wants to do that? Or, stop bathing altogether. Who really likes bathing anyway? Isn't there something nice about smelling like we humans were intended to smell? Like nature? Not convincing? Come on ... give it a shot.

Urban Bathing

Not ready to give up bathing altogether? Well, have you heard of Urban Camping? No? I'll summarize. It's basically just living rent-free in a tent wherever the hell you want. Pooping on sidewalks. Yelling at passersby. That sort of thing. Yeah, it's being homeless. Whatever! Call it whatever makes you feel better. Well, these urban campers often bathe—when the do bathe at all—in public facilities like the local pool. *That's* urban bathing. Surely your town has a pool or a fountain. Heck even a sink would do. Give it a shot, meet some new people, and save some money.

Stop Washing Your Clothes

Similar to bathing, washing your clothes uses a lot of energy without *that* much benefit. I mean, have you ever heard of anyone dying from smelling bad? I thought not. Plus, you'll be able to fit right in with those people living behind that building behind your house. So, stop washing your clothes and make some new friends.

Chapter 14: No lights? Let's Break Out The Batteries and Candle Wax.

How to prepare for a Black out

Most of us don't even think about the possibility of the electricity going out. We go through our lives sucking back the watts with an indifference to be marveled at, and only ever noticing the electricity when it flickers or when we get the bill every month. But, if you've ever been part of an electrical grid blackout, then you know they can be down-right scary. Imagine not knowing when you're going to be able to stream that next episode. It's a fucking nightmare. So, in this chapter we're going to help you avoid the nightmare ... or at least make it a little less terrifying.

Stock up on Supplies

A good way to approach this step is to think about what you would need if you went primitive tent camping. Everyone's idea of comfort is a little different, but here is a list of some of the basics:

- Lighting: Don't just think flashlights, here. There are a good variety of lighting options which can make a blackout pretty bearable. Fluorescent lamps and candles should be added to the list, and it's a good idea to have at least one in every room of the house.

- Ready/Nonperishable Foods: Miss those cans of ranch-style beans your wife won't let you buy anymore? Well now you have just the excuse you need. Make sure you throw some vegetables in there as well, and don't forget about fruit; you don't want to end up with scurvy.

- Battery Operated Radio: You'll want to make sure you can keep up with the latest information, and if the blackout lasts long enough, a radio is likely to last longer than your iPhone. Just make sure you know what station provides emergency information, and only run it for short periods of time.

Inspect your Generator

Oh, you don't have one. Shame on you! Go out and get a generator right now, and make sure it's sized properly. There are endless variations of these handy devices, and the one you buy needs to match the amount of use it is going to be responsible for. And if you do have a generator already, it is a good idea to check it at least once a year to make sure it operates properly.

Keep your Cellphone Charged

It's always a good idea to keep your cellphone charged during the day. You never know when you're going to be away from an outlet—or near one that doesn't provide any juice, in the case of a blackout—for a long period of time. And during a blackout, land lines are almost guaranteed to not work, so your cellphone might just be your only means of long-distance communication.

Know Where Everything Is

There is nothing worse than being in an emergency and not being able to remember where you stored the emergency supplies twelve years ago. Be sure to avoid this by setting a calendar reminder on your phone to refresh your memory (and your supplies) yearly.

Keep Ice Packs in your Freezer

In case the blackout stretches on for an hour or more, you'll want to have these available to keep perishables cool until the power comes back on.

What to do *During* a Blackout

Preparing for the blackout is like insurance. You hate that you had to purchase it, but you hope you never have to use it. But eventually, the chances are you'll experience a power outage. Now that you're ready for the nasty event, let's explore some ways to keep you safe and not too inconvenienced while it's ongoing.

Keep the Refrigerator Doors Closed

Most power outages only last for a few minutes to an hour. In these cases, your fridge should have enough cold air in it already to keep your food fresh until the lights come back on. In less common cases, where the power stays out for hours or days, only open the fridge doors when absolutely necessary, or not at all.

Run the Generator Outside away from Doors and Windows

Most generators are really loud, so just from a practical standpoint, you don't want them running anywhere near you, much less inside the house. Another—perhaps even better—reason to keep them outside while in operation is that if you don't ... you might die. Generators can emit large amounts of invisible poisonous gas known as Carbon Monoxide, and in high enough concentrations, this silent enemy can send you to your permanent blackout. So, have your generator professionally installed and located in a safe place.

Don't use your Stove to Heat your Home

Blackouts can be a cold affair during the winter months, and some unwilling participants might be tempted to use their gas stovetop to heat their frosted bunions. Avoid the urge! There are many reasons not to do this. Among them, the two main reasons are:

- Carbon Monoxide: Remember the silent killer? Using the gas stove on high for long periods of time can cause a buildup of the stuff and can leave you cold-dead.

- Fire Hazard: When *cooking* with gas, you generally remember to turn the burner off. But when heating your home with those burners, you might forget and leave them on overnight. This is just inviting your cat to jump up there and play in that pretty, sparkly stuff, and drag fire by the tail across your drapes. Just don't!

Disconnect Appliances and Devices

Sometimes a blackout can be accompanied by electrical surges. When these happen, even surge protectors can become overloaded and devices attached to them can get fried. You *just bought* that next-gen game console. Keep it safe! Keep it unplugged during a blackout.

Check on the Neighbors

I know they're not your favorite people in the world, but wouldn't you want them to do the same for you? I thought so. So, earn those neighbor points before they get the same idea, by checking in on them. It just takes a minute or two, and you might save someone's life. Or ... you could use it as an opportunity to scare the shit out of them by dressing up in Halloween garb and tapping on all their windows. That's probably a really bad idea in the South ... because of guns.

Head to a Shelter

If you find that your generator isn't working (despite checking it every month as discussed earlier), you might find yourself in need of some heat or cooling that you can't get at home during a blackout. Be sure you know the location of the local emergency shelters. They will have emergency backup generators and be able to keep you and your family air-conditioned. If you have pets, make sure you do your research and know which shelters will accept them. One benefit is you might actually get to know the neighbors that you've lived next to and been avoiding for these many years. Yay!

Chapter 15: Shockingly Funny Pick-Up Lines & Jokes

That's it. We're done. Go forth and save. Wait, you want more? You say, you're lonely and you want to try to pick up ladies while you're at the hardware store buying all this stuff, but you just don't know how to approach the opposite sex? You say you want to "wow" your friends with jokes based exclusively around electrical concepts and terminology? Well, you're in luck my awkward friend. Provided just for you, are—drumroll please— the best electricity-based jokes and pick-up lines.

Pick-up Lines

• Hey, sweetie. I had to come over and let you know ... every time I see you, it's like a switch gets flipped inside me. You really turn me on!

• Whoa there, little lady! Are you improperly grounded? Because when I stand too close to you, I feel a spark!

• You know, I just couldn't help but notice; you and I just seem so perfect together. You want to help me make a complete circuit?

• You can trust me; I'm an electrician. Now, let me remove your shorts!

• Baby you *must* be the secondary winding to my transformer. I'm feeling magnetically coupled to you.

• Hold on a second, sweetie. I just noticed something seems off. But don't worry, I know how to turn you back on.

• You must be putting out a serious charge, because something big is transforming in my pants.

• You may have felt the effects of electricity before, darling. But just wait until you get a taste of my high-voltage juice.

- Here, hold my cord.
- What are you doing later tonight? Why don't you come over to my place and you can help me re-wire my ham radio?
- Everybody else in the room is just putting out static, but your frequency is coming through loud and clear.
- Baby we're like a couple of live wires. Every time we touch, sparks fly.
- Hey there. I've got my wire-strippers. Want to get exposed?
- This conversation has had such a great flow, like a highly conductive alternating current with low resistance. Are you ready to see if my plug will fit into your electrical socket?

Jokes

- What kind of car does an electrician drive? A Volts-wagon.

- How did Benjamin Franklin feel after discovering electricity? Shocked.

- What does a barefooted man get when he steps on an electric wire? A pair of shocks.

- Sparky! Your mother and I are shocked at your current behavior. Until you learn to conduct yourself better, you're grounded.

- I finally managed to get rid of the nasty electrical charge I've been carrying. I'm ex-static!

- What do lightbulbs eat for fresh breath? A fila-mint!

- When I was young, I was afraid of the dark. Now, when I get me electric bill, I'm afraid of the light.

- What is an electrician's favorite flavor of ice-cream? Shock-a-lot.
- What did the single outlet say to the power-strip? Tramp!
- What did the baby lightbulb say to the mommy lightbulb? I love you watts and watts.
- My friend told me how electricity was measured, and I was like *watt*!
- What was the electrician detective's name? Sherlock Ohms. What was his sidekick's name? Dr. <u>Watt</u>son.
- My friend blew the power to the ice-making factory. Now they are heading into liquidation.
- Where do electricians get their supplies? Ohm Depot.
- My wife said the spark between us had gone out. So, I tasered her. I'll ask her again when she wakes up.

• My tight-fisted neighbor doesn't want to pay for an electrician to re-wire his house. "How hard can it be," he said. I think he's in for a bit of a shock.

• What do electricians chant when the meditate? Ohhhhmmmm.

• A superconductor walked into a bar. The bartender said, "Get out! We don't serve your kind here." The superconductor left without resistance.

• If you plant a lightbulb in your garden, does it grow into a power-plant?

• An electrician arrive home at 3 am. His wife asked him, "Wire you insulate?" He replied, "Watt's it to you. I'm Ohm, aren't I?"

• A chemist, a biologist and an electrical engineer had all been sentenced to death and were on death row waiting to go to the electric chair. Finally, the day had arrived. The chemist was due to go first. As he strapped him in, the executioner asked him, "Do you have anything you want to say?" The chemist replied, "No," so the executioner flicked the switch, but nothing happened. According to this State's law, if an execution attempt fails, the prisoner has to be released. So, the chemist was unstrapped and allowed to walk free. It was the biologist's turn next. As he was being strapped in, the executioner asked him, "Do you have anything you want to say?" The biologist replied, "No, just get on with it" so the executioner flicked the switch, but once again nothing happened. So, just like the chemist, the biologist was released. Then the electrical engineer was brought forward. The executioner asked him, "Do you have anything you want to say?" The engineer replied, "Yes. If you swap the red and the blue wires over there, you might just make this thing work."

• Paddy is talking to two of his friends at work. His first friend confides to the other two, "I think my wife is having an affair with the electrician. The other day I came home and found wire cutters under our bed and they weren't mine." The second friend then also confides, "Wow, me too! I think my wife is having an affair with the plumber. The other day I found a wrench under the bed and it wasn't mine." Paddy thinks for a minute and then says, "You know - I think my wife is having an affair with a horse." Both his friends look at him in complete disbelief. Paddy sees them looking at him and says, "No, seriously. The other day I came home early and found a jockey under our bed."

Chapter 16: High-Powered Trivia to Turn You On

Useless Facts about Electricity

Now that all your friends are amped up by your thorough collection of shocking jokes. *And* you have that new lady-friend on your arm, expertly secured by the armory of sizzling one-liners you employed. Let's keep the party going with some more, high-voltage information. In this chapter we'll charge you up with a smattering of interesting facts and mind-boggling records about electricity.

<u>Facts</u>

Electricity is some pretty amazing stuff, capable of things you might not have thought possible. From how fast it is, to how it behaves, share these facts at any party, and they're sure to light up the room.

- **Electricity is Fast:** In fact, it's the fastest known thing in the universe—

tied with light, of course—clocking in at 186,287 miles per second. To put that into a perspective that you probably can't actually imagine, if a lightning bolt were to strike out from the sun traveling at that speed, it would reach the earth—and probably destroy it—in only 499 seconds. This is also known as one astronomical unit.

• **It's also Very Strong:** A single spark of static electricity—like the ones that scare the shit out of you every time you open your car door in the winter—can measure up to three thousand volts. Good thing they are over in a hurry! And remember lightning? Those can reach up to three million volts and measure up to 54,000 degrees Fahrenheit! According to a website I just googled, forty such bolts, if properly harnessed with no loss of energy, could power the average household for a year.

- **Electricity Wants to be Grounded:** It's just the opposite of your snot-nosed teenage son. In fact, this is where the term "ground" comes from in the first place. You can most easily see this in a lightning storm. When you see that bright flash, chances are, it started in the clouds and ended up somewhere over the horizon. There are exceptions, of course, but electricity is always trying to find the ground. And as long as we stay out of its way, all is well in the world.

- **Electricity comes from Everything:** Well, not completely, absolutely, everything. But pretty much. You can make it by burning coal, spinning a turbine with water or the wind, collecting the energy from the sun, mixing specific chemicals together, or even from cow manure. It's as versatile as they come, and that's a good thing, because we humans have had an ever-increasing appetite for it ever since we learned how to use it.

• **It's in your Heart:** Electricity plays many vital roles in the body. One of these is to force your heart muscles to contract, sending that life-giving liquid to the rest of you. And if you've ever seen an ECG machine at a hospital, then you've seen this in action. Those devices, electrocardiograms, measure the electrical activity in the heart, and produce the little seismograph looking outputs on the screen.

• **Electric Animals:** Many animals harness the power of electricity for varying uses as well. Some sharks and other marine animals use it to find their prey. Most birds use it for navigation. Eels use it to shock things. Eels are such bad-asses! Even bees get in on the game, using small hairs to harness the information relayed in faint electric fields to help them find and pollinate flowers.

• **Gravity's Cousin:** Not really, but electrical fields do operate much like gravity. But where gravity only attracts, electrical fields can attract or repulse, depending on the polarity.

• **The Silent Killer:** Lightning is a sneaky bastard. In fact, if you get struck by the electrical ninja, you won't even hear it coming. That's because it moves faster than the speed of sound. But don't worry, contrary to popular belief, most of the time, people survive their encounter with lightning. Only about five hundred people per year get struck, and around ten percent, or about fifty actually die from it.

• **We Love Electricity:** Or, at least we love powering stuff with it. We've been using electricity to power things since at least as far back as the ancient Romans, believe it or not, and haven't stopped since. In truth, we've only increased our reliance. So much so, that the most recent estimate has us using 157,500 terawatt hours of electricity per year.

• **It can Teleport:** Sort of. Let's just say electricity is made up of tiny little particles, and those tiny little particles are made of even tinier little particles. The pieces get so tiny that they can't even be seen under a microscope. They have to be detected in some other sciency way. Well, those particles, the really tiny ones, can be on one side of a thing one moment, and then on the other side a moment later. Lots of smart people have tried to figure out how this happens, and so far, there are about twenty-five billion explanations. It's pretty much the same thing as *Beam me up, Scotty,* only one particle at a time, and completely useless. And uncontrollable. And invisible. And useless. But amazing!

• **It Doesn't Actually Flow:** I know, I know. I told you earlier that electricity flows, and I made this huge analogy to a river and all your buds in it. Well … I lied. It is still a helpful analogy, but in truth, electricity is way more complicated than simply flowing. What really happens is way too hard for me to explain accurately, but I've heard it described as more like a chain reaction within the electric wire. One piece bumps into the next piece, bumps into the next piece, until … magic. I like to think of it like dominoes tipping over. None of the dominoes actually go anywhere, but if looked at from far way, it does look a little like a "flow."

• **Tasers are Powerful:** The average taser emits fifty thousand volts of electricity. That's enough juice to burn or puncture your skin and cause the muscles of the body to contract so violently, that the tas-ee becomes completely incapacitated. Come on, you didn't think I'd have a section about electricity facts and not talk about tasers, did you?

• **The Electric Chair:** So, if a taser emits fifty-thousand volts and doesn't kill you, how many volts does it take to make you die? Actually, the answer is more about how long. You see, the taser zaps you and is over fairly quickly, leaving you relatively unharmed. However, an electric chair only uses about two thousand volts, but the current stays on for much longer, upwards of several minutes in some cases. This prolonged exposure causes lots of things to go wrong inside the body, and ultimately death. I'm no expert, but I'm guessing this is similar to how a person can be struck by three million volts of lightning for a split second and still survive about ninety percent of the time.

Records

With something as powerful and awe-inspiring as electricity, one would assume there are some pretty cool records surrounding it. One would be right. Kick back and peruse this list of incredible electrical records.

- **Invention of the Light Bulb:** Thomas Edison was a pretty cool dude. During his life he invented more than two thousand new products, many of which still help us use electricity today. He also built and owned the first power plant in New York City in 1882. One thing he did not invent however was the light bulb.

- **Discovery of Electricity:** Benjamin Franklin was a pretty smart dude, himself, though many erroneously attribute the discovery of electricity to him. Nope. We humans have known about the stuff for a lot longer than that. Evidence even suggests that the ancient Greeks, Romans, and Persians had discovered ways to use electricity for lighting, *and* in the process of making weaponry. Crazy! Benjamin Franklin did, however, discover that lightning itself was nothing more than a huge amount of electricity.

• **Most Powerful Power Station:** Power stations, also known as power plants, generate and provide electricity by burning fuel, rotating a turbine, harnessing nuclear power, or through many other methods. Without them you would be stuck in a continual blackout and have to resort to reading by firelight for entertainment after the sun goes down. And of all the power plants in the world, the most powerful is the Three Gorges Dam in China. This station provides hydro-electric power, and in 2014, produced a record 98.8 terawatt-hours (TWh). It supplies nine provinces and two cities, including Shanghai, with electricity. Are you surprised this record isn't held by a nuclear power plant? Don't be. Of the top ten most powerful stations in the world, only one was nuclear. The other nine? You guessed it—hydro.

• **The World's Brightest Flashlight:** Bright lights is a bit of an arms race, with companies outdoing each other seemingly every year. Their output is measured in lumens, and don't even think about using these contenders for any practical purpose. Unless you have a need to light up the bottom of the Mariana Trench, then stick to the offerings at your local hardware store. At the time of this writing the brightest flashlight in the world, measured in at a whopping 108,000 lumens. That's a lot of power. It drains its own batteries in less than ten minutes, and after six minutes, it's too hot to be held by hand.

By comparison, a standard, very-bright torch for camping use might top out at around twenty thousand lumens. But don't let the current record impress you; plans are already in the works for new models which could clock in at 160,000 lumens!

• **Invention of the Electric Car:** You may think that electric cars are a modern invention, but in fact, they are actually from the industrial age. The first electric car was built by American inventor William Morrison in 1891. It wasn't a big hit, as you can imagine; it's barely catching on even now. He did go on to invent something that he is much more famous for, however—the cotton-candy machine.

• **Longest Voluntary Self-electrocution by a Television:** Now, some people don't seem to understand the proper relationship between electricity and mankind. Daryl Learie is one of them. This man used a television to shock himself with 45,000 volts of electricity for 3.67 seconds. What's more? You can watch him do it. That's right, google that and enjoy. And wince. But still enjoy.

• **Longest Continuously Running Light Bulb:** Meet, the Centennial Bulb. Maintained by the Livermore -Pleasanton Fire Department, in Livermore, California, this light bulb has been running since 1901. 1-9-0-1! That's a long damn time for a light bulb to run without exploding ... or cracking ... or something other than working. But there it is, lighting up the air and giving power to our hopes and dreams ... or something.

• **Brightest Animals:** So now you know that animals use electricity for a variety of purposes, but did you know that some animals actually light up like a light bulb. If you grew up in the south of the United States, then this comes as no shock to you, but unfortunately those lightning bugs, or fireflies, depending on which state you're from, are not the brightest bulbs in the store. In fact, the most luminous animal of all is … we don't know. It's kind of hard to measure, and these animals don't really like to hold still, but we do think it is likely something in the jellyfish family. Not very exciting? Sorry, it's the fireflies then, totally the fireflies.

Conclusion

Electricity sucks, and electricity is awesome. It is a complete asshole, and yet it is very generous. Most of us know very little about it, though we all use it every day of our lives. Our relationship with the stuff has spanned several millennia, however even today we continue to take great strides in our understanding and application of it.

It powers our homes, and powers our hearts. It can shock our fingers, or kill us in a cornfield. We cook with it, clean with it, drive with it, and brush our teeth with it, and every year we use it more.

I hope this book has made you laugh, and made you pause. I hope it has brought you a better understanding of the juice that flows through your walls, and into your light bulbs. I hope you came here with an open mind and left with a lot of laughs. But most of all, I hope

you learned how to save a little bit of money
on electricity.

Bonus Methods

Hah! Just when you thought you were done, we surprised you with some more tips on how to save money on your electric bill. Read on, my tenacious friend.

Use a Push Vacuum

This is a lot like that reel mower we mentioned earlier. It may take a little more effort, but the reward will be well worth it. And, if you have rugs in your house, consider just shaking them out every now and then. That's how your ancestors did it, and they ... well, yeah, they probably had a much worse life than you, but still... They spent way less on electricity.

Replace the Automatic Garage Door

A basic rule of thumb is, if it's loud, it's probably also using a lot of electricity. And that applies to pretty much every garage door opener I've every heard. But it doesn't have to be that way. Just replace that noisy portal with a motorless one and hand crank your way in and out. You'll be saving money on electricity and beefing up your arms.

Do Chores at Night

A lot of electricity companies charge more for electricity during peak hours. Doing basic chores that use your highest-consuming household appliances at night, can save you some money. Some appliances have timers that you can use to schedule when they run, but who has money for that shit. Just plan some all-nighters like you used to do in college, and instead of going out drinking (when you were supposed to be studying), wash those dishes. Your house-mates probably won't love you for the extra noise, but fuck 'em—you're saving money god-damn-it!

Plug in at Work

These days, most people are carrying several devices with them everywhere they go. Phones, smart watches, portable speakers, wireless ear-buds—the list goes on and on. Many of these devices only have about one day of juice to a full charge, so instead of charging them overnight while you sleep, why don't you take them up to work with you and charge them on your boss's dime? He's got a lot of dimes. This is basically like giving yourself a raise without having to ask for it. You've been working hard. You deserve that raise! Now, if you're really adventurous, see if you can get some portable appliances to fit in your office and do your laundry there. Maybe even store some food? You normally eat there anyway, right? It could work...

Stop Googling

I know, I told you to google a bunch of shit already. How about this—only google-search ways to save electricity. "Why," you ask. Googling uses a bunch of electricity. A single google search is estimated to consume enough energy to turn on a 60-watt light bulb for seventeen minutes. Now that isn't all *your* energy, granted. Much of that is being burned off by the giant servers in at google-world. But still, any savings is good savings, right?